IN THOUGHT,

BY

MIKE MANAHAN

Edited by Daniel Welsh

Createspace

Table of Contents

Testimonials

For many years, God has reached out with His
love, touching my heart and soul with a timely message through
inspirational poems written by Mike Manahan. As I go about my
daily routine, one of God's words from these poems will come
to mind or I will sit for a while and read, finding the comfort
and direction my heart was crying for at that moment in time.
Our amazing God will use his poems to comfort me, heal my soul,
and strengthen my mind and heart. Then the Lord will use the
same words to cut through self-deception, deliver from times of
fears and calm my mind of confusion.

As you take this collection of poems, written by divine
inspiration, open your heart to God as He meets you face to
face. In simplicity of word and message, divine wisdom will
envelope you richly. Like a little child full of faith and
belief, call on the Lord with your whole heart and you will meet
the lover of your soul as He fills you with revelation, truth
and the refreshing purity of His Great and personal love.
His all-encompassing Love sent just to you.

-Janis

Mike Manahan continues to be amazing in his ability to take the world around us and express it so poetically. His insight and discernment enables the reader to visualize the topics Mike shares. Like a painter painting, his poems illustrate his message with clarity. You can see his heart at every word. I have received blessing after blessing watching Mike touch so many with his words of grace, mercy and most of all the love of the Father. His words of encouragement and enlightenment will speak to your heart. I encourage each of you to let his words speak to you!

-Ron Vunkannon

Introduction

When I was thinking about how I would put some poems together, I had recognized that they were very thought provoking and others had similar comments about the content of what I write. Sometimes when poetry is read, people tend to read it several times, just to see if they can get it to flow in a rhythmic fashion and that is a great way as well to let the content slowly seep into our soul, helping us to see a different perspective than we might have had before. So I thought that I would give the reader an option to journal their thoughts and what the poems might move them to change in their life. Change, I am sure would generally not come unless somehow challenged by the scriptures; thus, the format and title of the book, In Thought, Word and Deed. I hope you will find comfort, peace and joy as you read each poem as if the Lord wrote it directly to you.

THOUGHT

Your personal inspirational and emotional response to the poem

WORD

Related scripture verses that the poem brings to mind of the

reader

DEED

Actions to be taken or changes to be made in your life as the result of meditating on the THOUGHTS and WORD which were inspired by reading each individual

Abandoned

Have you ever been abandoned
Left by someone who cared
There's no other feeling so sad
And none that could make you so scared

Everyone knows what it's like
At least from their point of view
But nobody felt it like Jesus
So He can relate to you

He hung on the cross for hours
All of His friends walked away
No one could ever imagine His pain
As He gave His life that day

I'm sure that one by one they left
Each one not knowing the cost
Cause Jesus took all our pain on Himself
As He suffered upon that cross

I know that we'll never erase the sorrow
Or the ache when we're left alone
But Jesus can comfort in every way
And He will sow joy where sadness was sown

But we've got to look past the rejection
As Jesus looked past the cross
With joy in His heart, He endured the pain
Not seeing desertion as loss

Personal Notes

THOUGHT

_____

_____

_____

_____

_____

WORD

_____

_____

_____

_____

DEED

_____

_____

_____

_____

Chasing the Wind

Are you chasing the wind
All that you do seems in vain
Purpose has left you and you're all alone
Sitting naked and cold in the rain

Well, you're not alone in your situation
The Lord hasn't left you to drown
You just have to keep walking by faith
Cause He'll never let you down

And even when it seems as though
Hope is so far away
God is always by your side
And He'll be there to say

Trust in me, be not afraid
Just keep walking along
And soon you will find you've not lost your way
In your weakness, I'll make you strong

So even when you seem to be lost
And there is nowhere else to turn
Keep chasing the wind of the Spirit
And follow His every word

Then you'll be led by the Most High God
And you won't have to fret any more
Jesus will carry your worries and woes
And on the wind of the Spirit you'll soar

So trust in Him, be not afraid
Keep seeking and walking along
Soon you will find He will give you the faith
And in your weakness, He'll make you strong

Personal Notes

THOUGHT

_____

_____

_____

_____

_____

WORD

_____

_____

_____

_____

DEED

_____

_____

_____

_____

Anger on the Loose

Anger, anger, where have you been
Locked up deep inside
Where no one else has ever seen
Right there by my side

You come out when I'm all alone
And no one else can see
But when you rear your ugly head
I know that I'm not free

Anger, anger, you've been caught
One too many times
Here's a lesson I've been taught
To stop your evil crimes

As soon as I can recognize
That you are on the loose
I just repent and realize
Your neck's inside the noose

And then I think of things above
Not on things below
On things eternal, hope and love
So anger, you'll just have to go

Now I'll sing and praise the Lord
For showing me the way
Cause now I have a great reward
Peace and patience came today

Personal Notes

THOUGHT

_____

_____

_____

_____

WORD

_____

_____

_____

_____

DEED

_____

_____

_____

_____

Dark Thoughts in Paper Boats

Every thought that comes to mind
Must be carefully weighed
Because some can hold us captive
To make us so afraid

Some thoughts come from far away
And some from very near
But each of us has power
To cast down every fear

All the dark and musty thoughts
That crowds our minds each day
Come to us in paper boats
That we could blow away

And even though there are some things
That seems to sound OK
We must consider what we hear
Or our minds will soon decay

So try to see those paper boats
With eyes from up above
They're only lies from Satan,
Just trust God's grace and love

Personal Notes

THOUGHT

_____

_____

_____

_____

_____

WORD

_____

_____

_____

_____

DEED

_____

_____

_____

_____

Guard Your Heart

Every morning I wake up
The Lord is on my mind
But then as time goes by
Another way I find

I tend to let the world
Enter to control
And everything I see and hear
Moves into my soul

It brings in all the evil
To crush and tear apart
My eyes and ears you see
Are windows to my heart

And all I put before them
Flows in to have its way
Squeezing every ounce of life
And spreading its decay

But God has given words of truth
To guard my heart from fear
Protection from the evil one
Who always seems so near

The truth is that I have the power
To keep out hurt and pain
I've got to keep the windows closed
Until the Lord brings rain

Cause when He reigns within my heart
His fruit will always grow
I'll open up and let Him in
And from my heart He'll flow

So I'll guard my heart with all my might
And God will see me through
He'll give me ears to hear His word
And eyes to see His truth

Personal Notes

THOUGHT

WORD

DEED

Rend My Heart

Help me Lord to understand
What it means to rend my heart
I give my life into Your hand
The only place I know to start

I'll draw near and so will You
To find out what I need to do
To cleanse my hands and purify
My heart and mind from every lie

I only need to think Your thoughts
Remind me of the fight You fought
And thank You Lord for giving me
The keys to make the devil flee

When I submit and turn to You
Your patience You will show
Then I'll understand Your love
And how Your mercy overflows

Yes, I'll draw near and so will You
You'll tell me what I need to do
To cleanse my hands and purify
My heart and mind from every lie

I'll start to think Your thoughts, not mine
And only do what's on Your mind
I'll start to think Your thoughts, not mine
And only do what's on Your mind

Personal Notes

THOUGHT

_____

_____

_____

_____

_____

WORD

_____

_____

_____

_____

DEED

_____

_____

_____

_____

Tempered Like Steel

When trials come against you
And every test seems tough
Remember that the word of God
Is more than enough

For we know that temptation
Is only for a season
And God will strengthen every heart
Who sees the perfect reason

That even though affliction
May not come from Him
He uses it to make us strong
So we'll be fit to win

Tempered like a rod of steel
That's how we should be
So adversity won't hurt us
Cause we'll have eyes to see

That the fire that seems so hot
Can reinforce our love
So when each snare of hate returns
God's word will be enough

Enough that our response will be
The same that Jesus gives
He always acts with charity
And when we do we live

We live the life that Jesus gave
When He gave His life for all
Remember that compassion
Can keep us from a fall

Let's keep our armor on my friend
So when those trials come
We'll stand the test like tempered steel
When we respond in love

Personal Notes

THOUGHT

_____

_____

_____

_____

_____

WORD

_____

_____

_____

_____

DEED

_____

_____

_____

_____

Tested

Whenever you're tested
You know that it's wrong
To say why me Lord
I'm just not that strong

Because testing is not
From the Lord of the Heavens
It starts with our weakness
Like a wee bit of leaven
Lusts of the flesh
And desires for things
Draw us away
Until sin it will bring

And when sin is conceived
Death is not far behind
Cause reaping and sowing
Is the law we will find

If we sow to the flesh
Corruption will come
And our minds will be set
On the wrong we have done

But if by the Spirit
We seek things above
Life and peace will be ours
In the arms of His love

So don't allow anything
No matter how small
To draw your attention
Away from your call

To worship the Lord
In all that you do
And constantly seek Him
For His point of view

And then you will find
He desires to bless
All who will trust Him
Through every test

Personal Notes

THOUGHT

_____

_____

_____

_____

_____

WORD

_____

_____

_____

_____

DEED

_____

_____

_____

_____

The Dungeon of My Ego

I'll take you for a journey
Where it's dark and cold and dreary
Where the Son has rarely entered in
And thoughts are always weary

Down past all the memories
Of good times that we've had
Down into that lonely place
Where most things turn out sad

Down into that dungeon
Of ego and conceit
Where everything begins with me
And ends up in deceit

Always thinking of myself
And what will lift me up
Never concentrating
On mercy, grace and love

What can free me from myself
And all my selfish pride
That lurks down in that dungeon
Where anger hurts and cries

I've got to find a treatment
A perfect remedy
I know that I can't free myself
From all that's wounded me

But I know that God forgave me
For every wicked deed
And if I forgive the ones
Who hurt and crippled me

He'll heal those parts down deep inside
That only He can see
Releasing me from pride and ego
Giving victory

Personal Notes

THOUGHT

_____

_____

_____

_____

_____

WORD

_____

_____

_____

_____

DEED

_____

_____

_____

_____

Arms of Fear

When I was a little child
I had so many fears
And even now that I'm a man
And some things changed
Throughout the years

I still know that
A fear can be
More harmful
Than calamity

A fear can stop a work of art
A fear can stop a prayer
A fear will stop most anything
It really doesn't care

It terrifies the greatest man
It kills our goals and dreams
It grabs our heart so tight it hurts
And fills us full of silent screams

But God has given us a way
To silence every fear
It's written in His word you know
Just take the time to hear

His word will give us faith to live
His word will bring us light
His word will give us eyes to see
In the darkness of the night

But every fear that grips us
Has arms and hands that bind
And each one must be crucified
One finger at a time

Then peal them off and bury them
When each one gets exposed
And soon we'll find we're free at last
Free from all our fears and woes

Personal Notes

THOUGHT

_____

_____

_____

_____

_____

WORD

_____

_____

_____

_____

DEED

_____

_____

_____

_____

Changes

Every time I stop to think
Of where I could have been
I think of all the changes
I should have made and then

I see how much afraid I am
Of changes I should make
But then I hear the Father say
That what I give, He'll break

And what is broken multiplies
Like seeds in fertile ground
That hard shell has to crack you see
Before the fruit abounds

Cause after all its fruit we want
No matter what the cost
And just before a seed can grow
It seems as if it's lost

So don't you be afraid of change
Just boldly stand your ground
Don't hide when it begins to rain
That's when you grow I've found

The Lord knows what's in store for us
And He will make a way
He'll prepare a road for us
And lead us every day

His love will never fail me
And when I'm feelin' down
He shows me that it's for my good
He's hidden me in fertile ground

Personal Notes

THOUGHT

_____

_____

_____

_____

_____

WORD

_____

_____

_____

_____

DEED

_____

_____

_____

_____

Fearful Heart

So you say that fear has gripped your heart
With troubles and woes you can't face
Well I know that the enemy plans his attack
To discourage our soul and steal our faith

But there's a solution in every case
For the worry and fright that invades
We've got to stand with our minds prepared
To finish the fight and complete the race

For the Lord never said we could stroll right along
And trials would never be yours
But what He did say was be of good cheer
I've overcome the world

Then we'll overcome by the blood of the lamb
And our words of integrity
Will honor the Lord in all that we say
And in all that we do, we'll believe

We'll bring down the strongholds that grip us so tight
And conquer the fears of our soul
Until every worry that creeps in the night
Comes under the Spirit's control

Cause we know that the Lord gave us faith to quench
All the fiery darts of our foe
But we've got to believe and trust in His word
And give Him complete control

Personal Notes

THOUGHT

_____

_____

_____

_____

_____

WORD

_____

_____

_____

_____

DEED

_____

_____

_____

_____

I Believe in You

So many times
I say I can't do that
It's too hard for me

I've never really tried it
You don't know where I'm at
O Lord, can't you see

But so many times
I hear His voice so clear
O son, you are free

You're free to try
His words ring in my ear
Cause I believe in you
I believe in you

For I have chosen you
And I have placed within
Everything you'll ever need
To go and fight and win

You're precious in my sight
Empowered by my might
Guided by my light
Through the darkest night

So don't be so afraid my child
To do what I have said
I've given all there is to give
Now go where you've been led

For everyone who lives in me
Will be the light of men
You have the power to set men free
That's the reason you've been sent

Personal Notes

THOUGHT

WORD

DEED

Make Me a Lion

So many times I've been afraid
To tell about your mercy
I need your hand for courage Lord
I want to be set free

Your goodness always helps me see
Where I have fallen short
Your grace will help me overcome
I need your hand for courage Lord

So Lord, make me a Lion
Bold to speak your word
Make me strong and fearless
Totally assured
To go where I have never been
To say what you desire
To do the works that Jesus did
Lord set my soul on fire

I want to see your hand go forth
I want to see your power
I want to see your mercy Lord
Come to us this hour

So we will all be bold to speak
And in your might proclaim
Your kingdom Lord will rule and reign
Lord Jesus touch our hearts today
To make us all like lions
Bold to speak your word
Strong and ever fearless
We'll hold your hand assured

We'll go where we have never been
To say what you desire
We'll do the works that Jesus did
To set the world on fire

And then we'll see your mighty hand
We'll see your power too
We'll see your mercy to our land
Lord, help us be your truth

Personal Notes

THOUGHT

_____

_____

_____

_____

_____

WORD

_____

_____

_____

DEED

_____

_____

_____

_____

Shadows of the Enemy

Some folks say they've got it
Others just pretend to see
And some are bold enough to share
That shadows are their enemy

Shadows that deceive our eyes
And move us to believe
That they are something great to fear
With worries that they weave

They lurk in darkness near the light
And look so ominous
Larger than the real thing
But they can never harm us

Yes, we'll walk through the valley
The valley of the shadow of death
But the Lord said fear no evil
And laugh at Satan's threats

Cause God will never leave us
Even when we stray
So when you see the shadows
Don't fear and run away

For He is our protector
Our shield from the enemy
And He will show us how to walk
Through every shadowed valley

Remember He's a God of light
And we're His light on earth
So go and cast your shadow
Of healing and rebirth

Because the Lord knows what's inside
And He will give you light

Chorus:
Light to see the plan He has so clear
Light to take away the fear
Light to see when everything is dim
Light to help us see in Him

Personal Notes

THOUGHT

_____

_____

_____

_____

_____

WORD

_____

_____

_____

DEED

_____

_____

_____

_____

A Little Bit of Me - A Little Bit of You

Many times I've thought of life
As just a narrow road
And other times I've looked at things
So free that I would roam

But what I see most perilous
Is what comes in between
Cause that's what kills me day by day
The mixture within me

God doesn't like a little bit of me
Working with a little bit of Him
He wants all my heart and life
Then He'll give me strength to win

A little of the old
A little of the new
Will lead me down the garden path
And twist my point of view

It's so hard to be single minded
Seeing from His point of view
But with eyes from above He'll let me see
What glorious things He wants me to do

And all of the things this world can give
The things that are bad and even the good
If they're not the Lord I know they won't last
Cause they'll all be burned up like the hay and the wood

Cause God doesn't want a little of Him
Mixed with a little bit of me
He desires for me to live
Life abundantly

Personal Notes

THOUGHT

_____

_____

_____

_____

_____

WORD

_____

_____

_____

_____

DEED

_____

_____

_____

_____

Be a River

Once there was a little stream
Through the temple it came
Right next to the alter
It carried a holy name
As it trickled past the gate
I followed it beyond
Some of it flowed freely
And some stopped in a pond

The water that had stopped to flow
Had gone off on it's own
Now it had no way to go
It's wild oats were sown
But the water that moved in the way
Continued toward the sea
And it gave life to everything
It's banks were filled with fruitful trees

Trees whose leaves would never wilt
Whose fruit would always grow
They drank from holy waters
That from the temple flowed
The water is the Spirit
Flowing from the throne
The alter is our prayer life
Where seeds of life are sown

The river only flows as deep
As deep as we can pray
Most of us can see our feet
What more can I say
But every day we need to see
The waters rising higher
Until we're swimming in the Lord
And we've been set on fire

So don't allow your life to stray
And stagnate like that pond
We must continue in the faith
Then our Father will respond
He'll send us to the sea of men
To give His life to all
We'll bear His fruit forever
And our leaves will never fall

Personal Notes

THOUGHT

_____

_____

_____

_____

_____

WORD

_____

_____

_____

_____

DEED

_____

_____

_____

_____

Fire and Smoke

Lord I want Your fire
To burn within my Heart
So use Your fan to flame the spark
That's been there from the start

I know that life's not easy
And at times can be so tough
But with Your fire ablaze in me
Your grace will be enough

Enough to weather every storm
Enough to give me peace
Enough to give me joy complete
Captivity to sweet release

Cause all I know about You
Is mercy, love and grace
So pour Your oil upon my heart
Lord help me seek Your face

Personal Notes

THOUGHT

_____

_____

_____

_____

_____

WORD

_____

_____

_____

DEED

_____

_____

_____

_____

Hand in Hand

So many times I've asked the Lord
Why are you taking so long
Then I hear that small voice
Down deep in my Spirit
You've just got to hang on

Remember your past He says look unto Me
Get your eyes off yourself
You know deep inside, you cannot hide
You've got some secrets to tell

I will be here until you agree
You have to understand
If two want to walk together you see
They've got to walk hand in hand

So reach out for Me and not what I have
You need to see my heart
Every need and every desire
Have always been there from the start

And I've already given forgiveness in full
For everything you've ever done
But you've got to confess it right to my face
Then together we can run

We'll fly like the wind and never slow down
We'll ride on streams of light
But here is the key, together we'll be
Then you will see with my sight

And I will be here until you agree
You have to understand
If you want to walk together with me
We'll have to walk hand in hand

Personal Notes

THOUGHT

_____

_____

_____

_____

_____

WORD

_____

_____

_____

_____

DEED

_____

_____

_____

_____

Heart For the Harvest

How many people are starving
For food they know nothing about
How many people are dying
For life without worry and doubt

Everyone hurrying here and there
Trying to get to the top
Seeking the things that won't satisfy
Not knowing to go or to stop

But there is an answer to every dilemma
And obstacle coming our way
We've got to seek the Lord of the Heavens
And He'll give us peace every day

But what is important in His point of view
Is not just what bothers me most
He is concerned for eternity's goal
To save each and every soul

So give me a heart for the harvest
So I can be one with You
Yes give me a heart for the harvest
And a brand new attitude

Take away all of my selfish pride
And seeds of complacency
Then give me a heart for the lost and dying
One set on eternity

Oh give me a heart for the harvest
And nothing will hold me back
From doing Your will and choosing Your way
Lord fan Your flame in my lamp

Then oil me up on the inside
So I can burn clean and bright
Give me the tools to trim the wick
And I'll be ablaze with Your light

Personal Notes

THOUGHT

_____

_____

_____

_____

_____

WORD

_____

_____

_____

_____

DEED

_____

_____

_____

_____

Hide Me Lord

Lord I want to live
In your secret place
Hidden in your shadow
Behold You face to face

Then I'll be secure
And in Your love I'll be
Filled with strength and courage
Knowing that You're with me

So hide me Lord
Protect me from all harm
Shield me with Your wings of love
And hold me in your arms

Keep me in your secret place
Where evil can't intrude
And I will listen to your voice
In quiet solitude

Help me not to be afraid
When there's no one around
When there's no other voice
And no friends to be found

Just help me see
That place in You
Where only love abides
Where You and I are face to face
I'll have Your peace inside

Personal Notes

THOUGHT

_____

_____

_____

_____

_____

WORD

_____

_____

_____

_____

DEED

_____

_____

_____

_____

Mercy Man

Father, turn the tables of my heart
Chase away the money changers
Force them to depart

Then write upon the softened flesh
Your words of life I seek
Making me a mercy man
Filled with grace and peace

A mercy man, a mercy man
Is what I want to be
A mercy man, a mercy man
Strong and bold and free

Break those cold stone tablets
Filled with law and rules
Then fill me with a heart of grace
And use me as Your tool

A tool of mercy in Your hand
To break the bonds of strife
Give me words of mercy
That bring eternal life

A mercy man, a mercy man
Is what I want to be
A mercy man, a mercy man
Strong and bold and free

Lord, take away my judgement
And all my critical thoughts
Replace them with a heart of praise
And the mind that Jesus bought

Overflow my heart with love
So everyone will know
That You can make a heart of grace
From one that once was cold

And make of them a mercy man
Filled with grace and peace
A mercy man, a mercy man
Strong and bold and free

Personal Notes

THOUGHT

_____

_____

_____

_____

_____

WORD

_____

_____

_____

_____

DEED

_____

_____

_____

_____

Reading Mail

Can you imagine opening mail
Ever since time began
And finding all the secrets
Of every single man
Wouldn't it be difficult
To understand the words
Of someone you had never known
And never even heard

Would you find it hard to put yourself
In someone else's shoes
To see another person's life
From their point of view
And knowing that the day would come
When you'd meet them face to face
Could you forget the things they wrote
And show them love and grace

Well God's read everybody's mail
And in between the lines
He's read our hearts and still He says
I want you to be mine
And even though He knows us
Better than we know ourselves
He looks beyond our weaknesses
And takes us off the shelf
Cause He desires to use us
In every hour we live
To do the works of Jesus
He gave so we could give

Now when Jesus hung upon the cross
The Father turned His face
And Jesus said forgive them Lord
And gave us love and grace
So if the Lord's been reading your mail
And He's spoken to your heart
Respond to Him, He'll never fail
His love will never part
Cause God's read all our mail you know
And in between the lines
He knows our hearts and still He says
I want you to be mine

Personal Notes

THOUGHT

_____

_____

_____

_____

_____

WORD

_____

_____

_____

_____

DEED

_____

_____

_____

_____

Sleeping Bitterness

In a vision, I saw a falcon
Flying toward the earth
Its talons strong and mighty
Quite an awesome bird
It flew in my direction
Diving oh so steep
Suddenly it grabbed me
Clutching round my feet

I asked the Lord, what did it mean
What was holding me
He told me that the falcon
Was bitterness at sleep
He said I'd have to drown it
Or face the consequence
Of living life unable to move
Caught without defense

Get ready for the battle He said
Mount up and take your sword
Make sure your armor's set in place
You're fighting for the Lord
The warfare will be bloody
I'll need my shield of faith
That bitter seed will not give up
Until it's in its grave
And so I place my bitterness
Upon the cross to die
Crucified with Jesus
Never more to lie
Because the truth of bitterness
Is just that it destroys
Everything within its path
Stealing peace and joy
So if you find that bitter roots
Have grown inside your soul
Drown them in the sea of light
And they will lose control
Then place them on the cross of Christ
Never more to live
And you'll be free within your heart
You've learned how to forgive

Personal Notes

THOUGHT

_____

_____

_____

_____

_____

WORD

_____

_____

_____

_____

DEED

_____

_____

_____

_____

The Veil

The day that Jesus hung
Upon a cross to die
Wasn't just an ordinary
Day for you and I

Much of all that happened
Was quite behind the scenes
Like the veil in the temple torn
That sacrifice would cease

God showed that in the rending
Of the veil that covered Him
That He was now revealing
All that He had been

The God of all the ages
Of comfort and of peace
Sacrificed His only Son
So we could be released

Released to be the holy veil
Hung between Heaven and earth
And the slightest breath of God Himself
Will move us to be sure

Sure to speak His holy word
Sure to do His will
Sure to be His laborer
Working to rebuild

So be prepared to listen to
The whisper of the Spirit
Cause when He speaks so softly
You know you'll want to hear it
So you can be a blessing
To all who are in need
A vessel to be used of God
A veil pure and clean
But just remember every veil
Must be rent in two
So everyone can see the Lord
In all we say and do

Personal Notes

THOUGHT

_____

_____

_____

_____

_____

WORD

_____

_____

_____

_____

DEED

_____

_____

_____

_____

Branded

Lord I want to understand
The price You paid for me
Help me fully comprehend
The love that set me free

Give me more of what You are
So I can love like You
Then everyone will see
By everything I do

That I've been branded
I've got the mark of God
I've been branded
With a love that burns so hot

That I've got to give
Give it away
To everyone who longs
To see the price You paid

Yes, I've been branded
With the love of God
I've been branded
Now I know the cost

So fill me now with more of You
That everyone will see
The brand of God upon my life
Can set them free

Free to see the love You gave
When You died for all the lost
Giving freedom to the captive
To be branded by the cross

So now I've got to give
Give it away
To everyone who needs to see
The price You paid

Personal Notes

THOUGHT

_____

_____

_____

_____

WORD

_____

_____

_____

_____

DEED

_____

_____

_____

_____

Dreaming

Dreaming of the things above
Thinking of Your grace
Pondering Your faithful love
I see You face to face

When I want to hear Your voice
And long to hold your hand
I know that I must make a choice
To do what You command

And in my dreams, You show me
Who I need to be
A man full of compassion
For everyone I meet

Cause life is short and everyone
Is hurting deep inside
All of us are torn in two
Afraid to live, afraid to die

We've got to grab hold
And never let You go
For You are light and life and love
And someone to behold

I love to dream of things above
And think of love and grace
I'll ponder of Your faithful love
And see You face to face

Personal Notes

THOUGHT

_____

_____

_____

_____

_____

WORD

_____

_____

_____

_____

DEED

_____

_____

_____

_____

Flames of Forgiveness

Burn your grudges with flames of fire
Your unforgiveness will flee
We must remember that we are forgiven
And then we will be set free

We need to see through eyes of love
Then we could really let go
And free all the ones we've held so long
Just remember we reap what we sow

When we don't release
That one who's done wrong
Then we'll be the ones in chains
And we'll be the ones who suffer the loss
Holding on to our grief and pain

So loose all the captives
And soon you will see
Forgiveness is yours
You'll be totally free

Yes we've got to release
That one who's done wrong
So we won't be bound in chains
And we'll be the ones who are healed
Letting go of our grief and pain

Personal Notes

THOUGHT

_____

_____

_____

_____

_____

WORD

_____

_____

_____

_____

DEED

_____

_____

_____

_____

Love in the Third Degree

Oh Lord bring your kingdom
Build it in my heart
Bring the life of your own son
And set my life apart

Then give me your anointing
So I can bless and heal
And Jesus will be glorified
It's His touch that we feel

Cause You're alive and working
To purify and cleanse
Every temple needs you Lord
And the Spirit that You send

For Your desire in me is love
To build each bridge so strong
So pour it deep inside of me
And sing in me your song

A song of love that reaches out
To touch and lend a hand
A song that draws each one so close
To obey what you command

And love is what you've spoken
In all our hearts to be
Cause You our God are love in us
Love in the third degree

First You took and blessed Your Son
In every heavenly way
Then You broke Him on the cross
And then gave Him away

So why should we desire less
Than like our Lord to be
We must be broken, blessed and given
That's love in the third degree

Personal Notes

THOUGHT

_____

_____

_____

_____

_____

WORD

_____

_____

_____

_____

DEED

_____

_____

_____

_____

The Past Won't Change

Are you waiting for the past to change
Well you know it never will
You've got to live in the now
You can't hope for yesterday
Only in tomorrow
Got to keep your hand to the plow

All those hurtful memories
That haunts you every day
Every wound within your heart
And all your grief and pain

Was carried by the Son of Man
As He hung upon a tree
Suspended there upon a cross
He died for you and me

He knows what we're going through
And He knows where we've been
But He wants us to forget the past
Including all our sin

Cause God can't see our iniquities
Our sins are blotted out
All He sees is the blood of His Son
And He believes no doubt

That we can be free from days gone by
If we trust in His power and name
But we have to change our focus
For He will remain the same

Cause He knows what we're going through
And He knows where we've been
So we've got to forgive the things we've done
And forget about all our sin

Personal Notes

THOUGHT

_____

_____

_____

_____

WORD

_____

_____

_____

_____

DEED

_____

_____

_____

_____

A God Hearted Man

Some people it's said
Have a golden heart
They give and they give
Both near and far

But a heart of gold
Is not what I want
But the heart of the Lord
And the heart of my God

I want to be
A God hearted man
Faithful and true
And able to stand

When the going gets tough
And the battle is on
I will trust in the Lord
For He is my God

Yes a God hearted man
Is what I desire
To be in the times
When I'm in the fire

And a God hearted man
Is what I will be
Releasing His love
And living in peace

Personal Notes

THOUGHT

WORD

DEED

Tinted By the Blood

Lord, help me to understand
Forgiveness, forgiveness
Lord, help me see Your hand
Forgiveness, forgiveness

Show me a picture
Make me to see
How Your only Son
Could die for me

Cause all I know
Is how hard it can be
To look upon others
As You look at me

You see me righteous
You see me pure
You see me able
You see me secure
You see me healed
Delivered, redeemed
You see me whole beyond all my dreams

So now I will look
Upon everyone
As You look at me
Through the blood of Your Son

Cause You see us all
So righteous and pure
So able in You
And in You secure

Totally healed
Delivered, redeemed
You see us whole
Beyond all our dreams

I understand forgiveness now
It's how You see everyone
You look at us through rosy glasses
Tinted by the blood of Your Son

Personal Notes

THOUGHT

WORD

DEED

Warrior with Compassion

Lost on the front lines
Don't know what to do
I can't see tomorrow
Don't have a clue

I need Your direction
Your guidance to see
Which way to go
What You want me to be

I know that You love me
But sometimes I'm blind
Please come and heal
My heart and my mind

Then I'll be a warrior
Filled with Your grace
A soldier of compassion
Keeping Your pace

I'll follow Your Spirit
Walking in mercy
Doing Your will
Cause I know that You love me

Personal Notes

THOUGHT

_____

_____

_____

_____

_____

WORD

_____

_____

_____

_____

DEED

_____

_____

_____

_____

Glory in the Street

Oh Lord of the harvest
You know every heart
Please help us to see
Your plan from the start

We long to hear what You're speaking
To know Your every thought
We desire to see Your deeds
For it's Your face we've sought

We want Your power in the streets
So the ones who are needy will see
Your Glory coming down from above
Has been falling to set them free

Your anointing to break the bonds
That holds the captive so tight
Will truly release every prisoner
To see Your glorious light

Then all the nations will marvel
At what You've done by Your hand
And Your hope will be sparked in their hearts
To see You heal their land

Personal Notes

THOUGHT

_____

_____

_____

_____

WORD

_____

_____

_____

DEED

_____

_____

_____

God You are my Warrior

God You are my warrior
My defender and my guard
You have been there every hour
That's just who You are

Protecting me from foes without
And foes that are within
Helping me to walk in freedom
From all that I have been

You are my warrior
I trust in You
For You're my protector
I know You are true

You're true to Your word
I believe You will do
All that You've promised
For what I'll go through

Yes You are my warrior
You battle with me
We'll win together
And I will be free

Personal Notes

THOUGHT

_____

_____

_____

_____

_____

WORD

_____

_____

_____

DEED

_____

_____

_____

_____

More Than a Carpenter

Some say He was a carpenter
Just one who built with wood
Others say a teacher
Gentle, kind and good
Still others say a prophet
Who told of future times
A special man of history
Who spoke in riddles and rhymes

One who could deliver
With just a single word
A healer of the feeble ones
A man that many heard
But I believe He's more
Than just some carpenter
More than just a poet
Or some great orator

More than just a teacher
Who taught us right from wrong
More than just a gentle man
Kind and good and strong
More than just a prophet
Or healer of the lame
More than a deliverer
Jesus is His name

He is the only savior
This world will ever see
The firstborn from the Father God
Eternal prince of peace
Yes more than just a carpenter
Creating things with wood
For He can make a brand new man
Not just one that's good

And then He'll build the character
Until a man is strong
To overcome temptation
And sing a joyful song
So if you need to be set free
He's still alive today
Because you see He rose again
After the cross and the grave

Personal Notes

THOUGHT

WORD

DEED

What Does God Want

So many of us want to know
What others really want
Men really want to know
Really which restaurant

His girl or his wife
Would really enjoy
Or how does she really
Get truly annoyed

And women might need
To read a man's mind
When it's his birthday
And there's nothing to find

But how many of us
Want to know how God thinks
And what does He want
He is King of Kings

We just need to know
What He says in His word
Then get really quiet
It might seem absurd

But then you will hear
His voice deep inside
Down where His river
Can really abide

Then you'll know His thoughts
Intents and desires
And then you will know
That your soul is on fire

You'll know what He wants
For He never lies
He's always true
And His love never dies

Personal Notes

THOUGHT

_____

_____

_____

_____

_____

WORD

_____

_____

_____

_____

DEED

_____

_____

_____

_____

Control

When I think of all the things
I'm trying to control
My job, my friends and family
Most everything I know

Even things I cannot change
Or have some grand effect
I spend my time just thinking
Of exceptions to select

So much time is wasted
Attempting to command
And oversee the thoughts and deeds
Of everyone at hand

But now I see a different plan
Allowing God to rule
Let Him have dominion
And I'll just be a tool

I'll seek the Lord to move in power
And everyone will see
That I have given Him the reigns
And He has set me free

Now I'll praise Him for His might
And for His loving hand
I don't have to worry now
It's all in His command

Personal Notes

THOUGHT

_____

_____

_____

_____

WORD

_____

_____

_____

DEED

_____

_____

_____

_____

Fence Rider

Have you ever seen someone
Riding a fence
It's not very comfy
And doesn't make sense

To straddle the line
Between truth and a lie
Giving credence to one
And the other one hide

But most of us do it
Sometime every day
We compromise something
In some little way

We can't take rejection
So we smile and say
I really don't know
It looks kind of grey

Not really black
And not really white
Cause we've got to avoid
A conflict or fight

Now is that a life
That pleases the Lord
Throughout every day
In deed and in word

Or should we be truth
In a world full of lies
Giving God all the glory
Taking off our disguise

Personal Notes

THOUGHT

_____

_____

_____

_____

_____

WORD

_____

_____

_____

_____

DEED

_____

_____

_____

_____

Disciplined

So many things happen
In my life each day
It's hard to untangle the mess
Discerning what's God
Or the enemy's way
Is difficult I must confess

When trials come in
And worries persist
With afflictions on every side
I'll fight that deceiver
With all that I've got
Until all of the flesh in me dies

And whether it's discipline
Coming from God
Or Satan's schemes from below
Every response that comes from my life
Should be one that will help me to grow

So I'll stop all my whining
My anger will cease
Regardless of what comes my way
My God is the King
Of the whole universe
And He'll turn my night into day

His grace will abound in all that I do
For He has called me His son
I'll refuse to complain
And in all I'll obey
Until every victory is won

Personal Notes

THOUGHT

_____

_____

_____

_____

WORD

_____

_____

_____

DEED

_____

_____

_____

Grace to the Humble

Lord, You give grace to the humble
But the proud one isn't heard
Repentance and a softened heart
Will hear Your whispered word

We must continue to lean on Your might
And forever to trust in Your name
Remind us Father that You give us sight
Lord, teach us to trust and obey

And whether the road is smooth or rough
When I humble myself and give
My Father in Heaven with mercy and love
Will meet me where I live

So as long as His throne remains in my heart
I'll continue to hear His voice
When I humble myself, He'll set me apart
And I'll know I have made the right choice

Cause Lord You give grace when I'm humble
But when I'm proud, I'm not heard
So in repentance, I'll soften my heart
And I'll hear Your whispered word

Personal Notes

THOUGHT

_____

_____

_____

_____

_____

WORD

_____

_____

_____

_____

DEED

_____

_____

_____

_____

Rattle My Cage Lord

Have you ever had someone
Rattle your cage
Just shook you up
Till you disengaged

They took you out
Of your comfort zone
And just made you wish
That they'd leave you alone

Well God sometimes needs
To rattle our life
So our comfort zone
Will surely take flight

And if He is the rattler
We need to know
That what there is left
When He's shaped our soul

Is more of His light
And less dark in us
That we would change our
Unbelief into trust

So rattle my cage Lord
You know what I need
And You will bring me
Your life and Your peace

Personal Notes

THOUGHT

_____

_____

_____

_____

_____

WORD

_____

_____

_____

_____

DEED

_____

_____

_____

_____

89

Let it Rain

Is it raining in your heart today
Has everything seemed to go wrong
Well the Lord has the answer if you give Him your life
Cause He makes the weak to be strong

And who ever said that rain is so bad
Without it nothing would grow
You've just got to let His reign to come in
You have to give Him control

Then let the rain of His Spirit soak in
Let His mercy and love come down
Let the soil of your heart receive from Him
To grow in a heart of fertile ground
Cause sometimes there's only one way
To soften a heart so hard and dry
The tears of our life when the sky is so gray
Will someday bring us strength to fly

And after the Lord has watered our soul
He'll send His Son to shine
And if we will give Him control
He will give us peace of mind
So let the rain of His Spirit soak in
Let His mercy and love come down
Let the soil of your heart receive from Him
To grow in a heart of fertile ground

So if it's raining in your heart today
And everything seems to go wrong
Jesus has come to show you the way
And He'll give you strength to be strong

Then after He's watered your soul
God sends you His Son to shine
And when you give Him complete control
He'll give you peace of mind

So let the rain of His Spirit come in
And soften your heart to receive
Let His mercy and love come down
And you will be set free

Personal Notes

THOUGHT

WORD

DEED

One Nail at a Time

One nail at a time, that's how we should build
Molding the kingdom, a house from a field
Molding the kingdom, a stone at a time
United in purpose, One spirit, one mind

Remember the Lord, how He was not frail
Not using the sword, but receiving the nail

One nail at a time, one nail at a time
He kept His eyes on His Father above
Rejecting the lies, receiving the love

One nail at a time, one nail at a time
So we'll keep our eyes on the Father above
Rejecting the lies, receiving His love

One nail at a time, one nail at a time
Cause we died with Him, and in Him we live
He gave us His life so that we'd learn to give

And when we give, and die to ourself
His cross is glorified
Then He will give us strength to receive
One nail at a time

But what is the nail that we must receive
Heartaches and insults without a reprieve
And with all that the world or Satan can give
We'll joyfully look to the Father and live

For all that the Lord had to bear on the cross
Gave life eternal to all that are lost
For as He received one nail at a time
He paid the price for your soul and mine

Personal Notes

THOUGHT

_____

_____

_____

_____

_____

WORD

_____

_____

_____

_____

DEED

_____

_____

_____

_____

Rebuild the Ruins

Lord rebuild the ruins
The ruins of our hearts
Everything that's been destroyed
And all the broken parts

Father bring your Spirit
To search down deep inside
Help us Lord to understand
Our selfishness and pride

So Father we invite Your hand
To build new life and peace
Come and bring Your holiness
And Your power will increase

We know You need a willing heart
To mold and shape like clay
So Father we surrender all
Melt our hearts we pray

Personal Notes

THOUGHT

_____

_____

_____

_____

_____

WORD

_____

_____

_____

_____

DEED

_____

_____

_____

_____

Right or Wrong

I've been right and I've been wrong
But it doesn't seem to matter anymore
Cause what does it matter if you win the fight
If your attitude loses the war

We all have choices each day that we live
How to respond to every test
And I know that the Lord is standing so near
Hoping that we will abide in HIS rest
He is the sovereign, yes He's in control
He knows how it's going to end
He sees the bumps and curves in the road
But He sees the victory around every bend

Two wrongs don't make a right
I've heard it said before
And we must choose obedience
In following the Lord
And I know that the Lord
Would surely agree
The choice of obedience
Sets us free
So when have a choice between
Obedience or right
We've got to choose the one that shows
The Father's perfect sight
When the Lord healed a man on the Sabbath day
Some questioned if that was right
But He knew their thoughts and in His reply
He divided the darkness from light

Would you save a lamb if it went astray
No matter what day it would roam
This little picture would show them that right
Would never have brought that little one home
Remember that God looks upon your heart
And not upon circumstance
He wants us to be conformed to the Lord
And He is not subject to our demands
Yes we all have choices each day that we live
And how we respond to the test
Will tell us how close or how distant we are
To abiding in His rest

Personal Notes

THOUGHT

_____

_____

_____

_____

_____

WORD

_____

_____

_____

_____

DEED

_____

_____

_____

_____

Sifted Till You Win

Have you seen my servant Job
There's none like him around
God told Satan he could test
Cause Jobs the best that can be found
Now everyone knows what Job went through
Like no one else on earth
With boils and sores from head to toe
He cursed the day of his birth

So the devil was given power
To afflict in every way
He killed Job's sons and daughters
And his servants and sheep one day
He longed for death to come
And cried out in despair
For what he feared was his you see
He couldn't see God cared

Then Satan demanded permission to sift
Simon Peter was his name
Jesus prayed his faith would stand
This wasn't just a nine inning game
You play till you win
Cause the price was paid
With Christ on the cross
So don't be afraid
But can't you see that we're the same
And Satan's still the one to blame
He sifts us all each day you know
So just remember he's our foe
Cause God is on our side to win
To purify from every sin
And Jesus wants our faith to stand
Until we reach His promised land

So be content in everything
And sin not with your mouth
Cause what you fear within your heart
Will soon be yours no doubt
But you play till you win, and that's the rules
Cause Jesus paid the price for you
And all you really have to do
Is trust in Him and speak the truth

Personal Notes

THOUGHT

_____

_____

_____

_____

_____

WORD

_____

_____

_____

_____

DEED

_____

_____

_____

_____

Paper Soldier

A little paper soldier
Is what he made today
With his imagination
My son began to play

With paper, tape and clips
He made his little man
That was all he had to use
But he had quite a plan

Oh there were some frustrations
Some problems to resolve
But with patience and assurance
He saw them all dissolve

I wondered as I watched
How God imagined me
As He conceived His pattern
That a soldier I would be

There wasn't much to work with
Just a heap of clay
But He had full assurance
Of what He'd build by faith

He knew the blueprint well
For He understood my heart
There'd have to be the death of me
Before His plan could start

Then He could recreate me
As a warrior with His blood
He bought that lump of clay you see
With the life of His own Son

And I hope my son will understand
That what God needs to start
Is one who'll give Him everything
To get a soldier's heart

Personal Notes

THOUGHT

_____

_____

_____

_____

_____

WORD

_____

_____

_____

DEED

_____

_____

_____

_____

Wind in Your Face

I was walking on the beach one day
The wind was from behind
Didn't really notice much
Nothing on my mind

But when I turned around I felt
The breeze upon my face
My eyes began to water
And my steps had lost their pace

I now could hear it's whisper
And suddenly I heard
Through the wind God spoke to me
A message from His word

You must turn to hear My voice
And see through teary eyes
You have to slow your pace my son
To see the enemy's lies

I never heard His voice so strong
Or saw His plan so clear
The reason why I haven't turned
Is wrapped up in my fears

Fears of what He'd have me do
Fears of my response
Fears of men's opinions too
And fears of all my wants

Then He spoke these words to me
You need not be afraid
My love is for your good you see
And never ever fades

So now each time I feel the wind
I remember what He said
Just turn to Me and hear my voice
And by my Spirit you'll be led

Personal Notes

THOUGHT

_____

_____

_____

_____

_____

WORD

_____

_____

_____

_____

DEED

_____

_____

_____

_____

About the Author

Mike, as his friends and family call him, was born in Chicago, Illinois, 63 years ago. He is a graduate of West Virginia University, holding a master's degree in Physical Education. He has been coaching gymnastics for 43 years and has enjoyed his relationships in that field as well as in churches he has attended since his early 20's. He and his wife, Faith, live in Tallahassee where he has been the head men's gymnastics coach for Trousdell Gymnastics Center for the past 20 years.

Mike and his wife attend Lifepoint, a local church where they have enjoyed fellowship for the past several years. The messages in his journal represent flashes of wisdom and insight over the years. His love for writing has been inspired by everything from notes from pastors' sermons, to something that a commentator says on a football game, to driving down the road, just thinking about the Lord and how God wants to be a part of everything in our lives.

Made in the USA
Lexington, KY
22 February 2017